MY LITTLE RED BOOK

For Very Important Data

MY LITTLE RED BOOK

For Very Important Data

MY LITTLE RED BOOK
For Very Important Data

ISBN-13: 978-1-940961-40-8
ISBN-10: 1940961-40-8

Cover Art & Interior Layout Design created by Richard Voigt
All Original Artwork and/or Photos by Richard Voigt – aka RIVO
Publication collaboration, proof, editing & revisions by Lynn Voigt

First Printing 2017 – (RIVO Inc. – RIVO Books)
Printed in the United States of America

To Access Our Latest Publications & Marketing Tools Visit:

www.RIVObooks.com
www.RIVOinc.com

About The Authors:

Richard and Lynn are educational problem solvers that develop creative strategies that paint dreams, sell ideas, and market messages. Together, they present a unique team-approach, as project consultants working side-by-side with each client; utilizing their life-long skills and diverse expertise as motivational speakers, problem solvers, inventors, authors, artists, and education specialists.

Teaching by example, they focus on research and development, latest trends & technology, SEO, domain acquisitions, video production, and self-publishing advocates working on behalf of their company, RIVO Inc. – RIVO Marketing since 1997.

At the time of this publication, they have created and produced over 750 videos that have been viewed millions of times, quickly gaining tens of thousand subscribers from over one hundred countries around the globe.

They've self-published over 60 books on a wide of topics from self-help, motivation and inspiration, art, gardening, and Internet marketing. They also teach classes via the University of Wisconsin Osher program and Waukesha County Technical College, via the LIR program.

Their life-long mission as professional educators is to uncover new strategies, product and services, networking useful solutions for themselves and their clients, both online and offline, assist entrepreneurs, small business owners, writers, local artists, models, teachers and students helping them clarify marketing their products and services.

Feel free to contact them if you have questions or would like to tap into their talents and expertise. They truly appreciate your feedback and look forward to hearing your success stories.

Richard & Lynn Voigt - RIVO
Education Specialist

Website: www.RIVObooks.com
Email: support@RIVOinc.com